For Yoona, and all the other young curious minds.
It's okay to fall. You can always get back up and try again.

# Vera Wang

A Story of a Little Girl Who Became a World-Famous Fashion Designer

Yeonsil Yoo

In bustling New York City, there was a little girl named Vera Wang. Vera enjoyed ice skating so much that she spent hours practicing almost every day.

She loved the beautiful costumes, music, and graceful movements and dreamed of becoming a champion skater one day.

But even though she worked really hard for years, Vera couldn't make it to the U.S. Olympic figure skating team. She felt sad but knew it was time to try different things and find other passions.

When Vera was in college, she decided to spend time in Paris, France, to explore a different part of the world. In Paris, she discovered many different styles and beautiful things. Soon, she fell in love with fashion!

Naturally, Vera decided to work at a famous fashion magazine for her first job.

She learned all about fashion and wrote stories about the latest trends. With her creativity and hard work, she published numerous magazines that millions of people enjoyed.

Vera loved her job, but she aspired to create clothes, too. Although it wasn't easy to leave what she loved, she knew it was time to explore a new world, just as she had before.

So, she joined a big fashion company.

However, Vera faced new challenges. Her imagination had to align with the company's style and direction. She craved the opportunity to fully express herself and bring her unique ideas to life.

One day, when Vera was getting married, she searched for the perfect dress but couldn't find anything that felt right for her. So she decided to design her own dress just the way she wanted. She put her plan into action right away.

The dress was simple, elegant, and most importantly, it made her feel like herself.

Everyone loved it so much that Vera thought she could make beautiful wedding gowns for others too. It was definitely a scary idea, but deep inside, she knew she should give it a try.

So Vera opened her own store in New York City. She wanted to create dresses that made every bride feel special and beautiful on their big day.

Her unique designs quickly became so popular that many celebrities started asking her to make dresses for their weddings.

As Vera's bridal shop grew, she received many awards for her stunning designs. Her dresses appeared in various fashion magazines, TV shows, and movies. Vera's talent and dedication made her a true fashion icon.

But Vera didn't stop there. She took courage and expanded her brand to include eyewear, perfumes, ready-to-wear collections, and even home décor. Her small shop grew into a massive, international brand that many people around the world loved.

Over time, she learned to embrace and move through these challenges with joy.

Vera taught us that it's okay to be scared.
The important thing is to look forward, be brave, and try new things.

If some doors are closed, you can always get up and look for another door!

# The Story of
# Vera Wang

Little Vera, the Skater

Vera Dreaming of Joining the Olympic Team

Vera's Wedding Day

Vera Wang's journey in fashion didn't happen overnight—it was built on years of hard work and a willingness to try new things. After the disappointment of not making the Olympic skating team, Vera could have given up on her dreams. Instead, she sought out new passions, and that decision changed her life.

When her first bridal designs were praised, Vera didn't stop there. She knew success wouldn't come easily, so she continued to push boundaries,

Vera's First Bridal Shop in 1990

Vera's Beautiful Dress on a TV Show

Receiving the National Medal of the Arts

expanding her work into new fields like evening gowns, perfumes, and even home décor.

Her resilience paid off, and she became one of the most famous designers in the world, known not only for her stunning creations but also for her spirit of constant growth and learning. Vera Wang's story shows that when life takes an unexpected turn, staying strong and believing in yourself can lead to extraordinary achievements.

UPFLY BOOKS

© Copyright 2024 - Yeonsil Yoo, all rights reserved.
Paperback ISBN: 978-1-998277-45-2
Hardback ISBN: 978-1-998277-46-9

www.upflybooks.com

No part of this publication may be reproduced, stored in a retrieval system, or transmitted in any form or by any means, electronic, mechanical, photocopying, recording, or otherwise, without the prior written permission of the publisher, except as permitted under copyright law.

Photographic acknowledgments (pages 30-31):
Vera Wang's Instagram and X (@VeraWang)
Penske Media via Getty Images for Vera Wang's First Bridal Shop
Photo by Patrick Demarchelier, Vogue, June 2008, featuring Sarah Jessica Parker

# Other Books by the Author

Get Your Next eBook for FREE! Scan the QR code or visit upflybooks.com to sign up as a beta reader!

www.ingramcontent.com/pod-product-compliance
Lightning Source LLC
Chambersburg PA
CBHW061351010526
44107CB00011B/899